WELCOME TO THE
OLD
DEARS'
CLUB
Members' Handbook

This edition published in 2017
by Baker & Taylor UK Ltd
Bicester, Oxfordshire OX26 4ST

Text by Michael Powell and Fiona Thornton
Contents layout: seagulls.net
Cover layout: Milestone Creative

ISBN: 978-1-910562-88-8

Printed in China

WELCOME TO THE
OLD DEARS' CLUB

Members' Handbook

MISSION STATEMENT

THE OLD DEARS' CLUB

AIMS: to celebrate, represent, unify, protect, enhance, honour, empower, inspire, connect, protect, strengthen, enhance, serve, promote, manage, support, advocate for, espouse and recommend a nice sit down with a cup of tea and a plate of biscuits.*

When three or more old dears gather together, an old dear quorum is formed, so pop the kettle on and crack open a packet of chocolate digestives.

*To ensure the brevity of this mission statement, 'tea and biscuits' may be assumed to include any of the following: soft mints, hard mints, fruit cakes, corned beef, tinned soup, apple crumble, condensed milk, rhubarb, Victoria sponge, offal, syrup of figs, tinned rice pudding, glacé cherries, kippers, a nice tin of salmon, tinned peaches, ham hock, porridge, liquorice, meat pies, half a grapefruit and prawn cocktail, and shall be said to exclude 'any of that foreign muck'.

JOIN THE CLUB

Nice to be here? At my age it's nice to be anywhere.

Now I've learned the rules of life, I think I'll invent my own game.

'YOU CAN'T TURN BACK THE CLOCK BUT YOU CAN WIND IT UP AGAIN.'

Bonnie Prudden

KEEP YOUR ENTHUSIASM AND FORGET YOUR BIRTHDAYS.

NEVER THINK YOU HAVE SEEN THE LAST OF ANYTHING.

IT'S JUST A
NUMBER

'I do wish I could tell you my age, but it's impossible. It keeps changing all the time.'

Greer Garson

'I believe in loyalty. When a woman reaches an age she likes, she should stick with it.'

Eva Gabor

'SHE SAID SHE WAS APPROACHING FORTY – AND I COULDN'T HELP WONDERING FROM WHICH DIRECTION.'

Bob Hope

I'm not 60 – I'm just 50 plus VAT.

AGE DOESN'T REALLY MATTER;

WHAT MATTERS IS HOW LONG YOU'VE BEEN THAT AGE.

'SAY I AM SEVENTY-FIVE AND LET IT GO AT THAT.'

Marlene Dietrich

'LOOKING FIFTY IS GREAT - IF YOU'RE SIXTY.'

Joan Rivers

HEY, GOOD-LOOKIN'

'I've got everything I always had. Only it's six inches lower.'

Gypsy Rose Lee

'I don't plan to grow old gracefully. I plan to have facelifts until my ears meet.'

Rita Rudner

IT'S IMPORTANT TO HAVE A TWINKLE IN YOUR WRINKLE.

'AFTER FORTY A WOMAN HAS TO CHOOSE BETWEEN LOSING HER FIGURE OR HER FACE.

MY ADVICE IS TO KEEP YOUR FACE AND STAY SITTING DOWN.'

Dame Barbara Cartland

TIME MAY BE A GREAT HEALER, BUT IT'S A TERRIBLE BEAUTICIAN.

I'M SITTING HERE THINKING HOW NICE IT IS THAT WRINKLES DON'T HURT.

FOND MEMORIES

'WOMEN AND
ELEPHANTS
NEVER FORGET.'

Dorothy Parker

'HAPPINESS IS
GOOD HEALTH AND
A BAD MEMORY.'

Ingrid Bergman

JOAN: MY DEAR! CAN YOU EVER FORGIVE ME? I FORGOT TO COME TO YOUR PARTY ON SATURDAY.

DAPHNE: MY DEAR! WEREN'T YOU THERE?

NATURE ALWAYS HAS A REASON.

Women over fifty don't have babies because they would put them down and then forget where they had left them.

I know my secrets are safe with my friends, because at our age they can't remember them either.

I finally got it all together. I just forgot where I put it.

CLUB RULES

THE FIRST RULE OF OLD DEARS' CLUB:
You talk about the weather.

THE SECOND RULE OF OLD DEARS' CLUB:
You talk about the weather.

You must speak with frequent hesitation, repetition and deviation for at least eighteen minutes and your conversation should include:

a) observations about the weather at this precise moment

b) predictions about the weather in the near to medium future

c) a brief summary of preceding weather, followed by polite criticism (e.g. the disappointing summer)

d) wry acknowledgment of the increasing unpredictability of the changeable weather

e) doom-laden conjecture about how much more changeable the weather may become in the future

f) mutual agreement that 'at least it's not raining'

THIRD RULE OF OLD DEARS' CLUB:
Someone yells 'Stop!', suggests a nice cup of tea or opens a packet of Murray Mints, and the discussion is over.

WEATHER
WOES

I'M SO OLD I REMEMBER WHEN RAINBOWS WERE BLACK AND WHITE.

MY JOINTS CAN PREDICT THE WEATHER BETTER THAN ANY WEATHER FORECAST.

'IF THE TEMPERATURE IS LESS THAN MY AGE, I DON'T GET OUT OF BED.'

Ellen DeGeneres

PROFESSIONAL PROBLEMS

WHEN HAIRDRESSERS
GET OLD, THEY
DON'T FADE,
THEY DYE AWAY.

WHEN TEACHERS
GET OLD, THEY
LOSE CONTROL OF
THEIR PUPILS.

WHEN DOCTORS GET OLD, THEY LOSE THEIR PATIENCE.

When librarians get old, they go out of print.

When quilters get old, they go under cover.

WHEN VIOLINISTS GET OLD,

THEY BECOME UNSTRUNG.

WHEN FORTUNE TELLERS GET OLD, THEY LOSE THEIR VISION.

WHEN LIMBO DANCERS GET OLD, THEY START TO GO UNDER.

GRAND PARENTING

No, other people's grandchildren are NOT as cute as mine.

The writing's on the wall. Uh-oh, the grandchildren got hold of the crayons again.

Dear Grandma,

I'm sorry I didn't write sooner to thank you for the Christmas money. It would serve me right if you didn't remember my birthday on 31st March.

Love

Alfie

LITTLE GIRL: GRANNY, WHY ARE YOU PUTTING CREAM ON YOUR FACE?

GRANNY: IT'S TO KEEP MY SKIN LOOKING YOUNG.

LITTLE GIRL: IT'S NOT WORKING, IS IT?

'IF GOD HAD INTENDED US TO FOLLOW RECIPES, HE WOULDN'T HAVE GIVEN US GRANDMOTHERS.'

Linda Henley

'THE REASON GRANDPARENTS AND GRANDCHILDREN GET ALONG SO WELL IS THAT THEY HAVE A COMMON ENEMY.'

Sam Levenson

YOU'RE AS OLD AS YOU FEEL

'As a graduate of the Zsa Zsa Gabor School of Creative Mathematics, I honestly do not know how old I am.'

Erma Bombeck

'The years that a woman subtracts from her age are not lost; they are added to the ages of other women.'

Comtesse Diane

I FEEL YOUNG AT HEART

- BUT SLIGHTLY OLDER IN OTHER PLACES.

'I'M NOT DENYING MY AGE, I'M EMBELLISHING MY YOUTH.'

Tamara Reynolds

'A WOMAN HAS THE AGE SHE DESERVES.'

Coco Chanel

'IN A DREAM YOU ARE NEVER EIGHTY.'

Anne Sexton

'The great thing about getting older is that you don't lose all the other ages you've been.'

Madeleine L'Engle

NON-DISCLOSURE
AGREEMENT

Sign this Non-Disclosure Agreement to keep a lid on vital proprietary information of the old dear mind: the Ten Secrets You Will Take To Your Grave.

This agreement shall be delivered in the manner prescribed by old dear law as of the date first written: _____.

I, _____, promise not to tell anyone ten years younger than me how I really feel about this stuff. So help me up the stairs.

CONFIDENTIAL INFORMATION:

1. My grandchildren annoy me quite a lot of the time and my children take me for granted to supply free childcare on demand.

2. After turning sixty I didn't feel liberated. I felt breathless, unattractive and largely invisible.

3. I don't appreciate bath spa sets. I don't want to smell like shea butter and pineapples.

4. I wish my family would stop buying me poignant Irish novels.

5. Walking is pointless. I don't need healthful activity and I don't want to be a fitness ambassador.

6. I am fully aware of that huge mole with a thick black hair growing out of it. Ditto my moustache.

7. I am perfectly capable of applying lipstick without getting it on my teeth; I just choose not to.

8. Many struggles do not get easier with old age.

9. Sex doesn't get better; it just stops.

10. Young people didn't ruin everything; we already did that decades ago.

If it appears that the signee has disclosed or threatened to disclose confidential information in violation of this agreement, she will forfeit her tea and biscuit privileges.

SIGNED:_____

TAKING IT TO THE
GRAVE

'I don't want to achieve immortality through my work. I want to achieve it through not dying.'

Woody Allen

'I wouldn't be caught dead marrying a woman old enough to be my wife.'

Tony Curtis

WHAT DO YOU CALL A WOMAN WHO ALWAYS KNOWS EXACTLY WHERE HER HUSBAND IS, DAY OR NIGHT?

A WIDOW.

BODY IMAGE

You don't know real embarrassment until your hip sets off a metal detector.

Middle age is when a narrow waist and a broad mind begin to change places.

THEY SAY THAT AGE IS ALL IN YOUR MIND. THE TRICK IS TO KEEP IF FROM CREEPING DOWN INTO YOUR BODY.

'THE OLDER YOU GET, THE HARDER IT IS TO LOSE WEIGHT, BECAUSE YOUR BODY HAS MADE FRIENDS WITH YOUR FAT.'

Lynne Alpern

'The only parts left of my original body are my elbows.'

Phyllis Diller

'I've got enough crow's feet to start a bird sanctuary.'

Kathy Lette

WOMEN
OF A CERTAIN AGE

I COULD TOLERATE HOT FLUSHES MUCH BETTER IF THEY MELTED MY EXCESS FAT INSTEAD OF MY BRAIN.

IF SCIENTISTS FIND A CURE FOR MENOPAUSE SYMPTOMS, WILL THE WORLD SUFFER FROM GLOBAL COOLING?

I hate it when you offer someone a genuine compliment about their moustache, and then suddenly she doesn't want to be your friend any more.

As I sat slumped over the table this morning, I thought I was having a hot flush. Then I realised my boobs were in my coffee.

Don't think of it as getting hot flushes; think of it as your inner child playing with matches.

'ROCK AND MENOPAUSE DO NOT MIX.'

Stevie Nicks

IT'S NOT A HOT FLUSH, IT'S A POWER SURGE!

MY HOT FLUSH JUST SET OFF THE SMOKE ALARM.

FIGHTING FIT, OR FIGHTING FITNESS?

Enjoy keeping active. Remember – if you rest, you rust.

I don't exercise because it makes the ice jump right out of my glass.

I JOINED A SENIORS' EXERCISE CLASS. I BENT, TWISTED, GYRATED, JUMPED UP AND DOWN AND PERSPIRED FOR AN HOUR.

BUT BY THE TIME I GOT MY LEOTARD ON THE CLASS WAS OVER.

BLESSED ARE THEY WHO HUNGER AND THIRST,
FOR THEY ARE STICKING TO THEIR DIETS.

'WHENEVER I FEEL LIKE EXERCISE, I LIE DOWN UNTIL THE FEELING PASSES.'

R.M. Hutchins

'I exercise every morning without fail. Up, down! Up, down! And then the other eyelid.'

Phyllis Diller

'I don't exercise. If God wanted me to bend over, he'd have put diamonds on the floor.'

Joan Rivers

THE OLD DEAR
PROMISE

The Old Dear Promise reflects the beliefs and attitudes that every old dear should strive to uphold:

On my honour,
I promise that I will do my best
to uphold our Old Dear values,

- to sleep whenever I am stationary

- to wake when my bladder tells me

- to put the kettle on persistently

- to always wear a sweater in July

- to wear grey pleated skirts with an elastic waistband

- to do my duty to daytime television

- to never own a pet I can't carry

- to always keep a spare tissue up my sleeve

- to listen to audio books

- to walk slowly along pavements and supermarket aisles

- to count out the exact change, slowly, even when there's a queue behind me

- to enjoy folding laundry

- to complete at least ten crossword puzzles every week

- to remind everyone that 'all this used to be fields'

and always to keep the Old Dear Law.

IN THE GOOD OLD DAYS...

... television finished at ten o'clock.

... your tights came in two pieces.

... YOU NEVER LOST YOUR CAR KEYS - YOU JUST LEFT THEM IN THE IGNITION.

... A SPANIEL CROSSED WITH A POODLE WAS A MONGREL.

... YOU HAD TO CARRY CHANGE FOR THE PHONE BOX.

DRESSED TO IMPRESS

I'M NOT WEARING A WONDERBRA. I'M WEARING A 'WONDER WHERE THEY WENT?' BRA.

IF I SEE SOMEONE WEARING CAMOUFLAGE I WALK RIGHT INTO THEM. I WANT THEM TO KNOW IT WORKS.

My birthday suit needs regular ironing.

DORIS: WHENEVER I'M DOWN IN THE DUMPS, I GET MYSELF A NEW OUTFIT.

FLO: REALLY? I WONDERED WHERE YOU GOT THEM FROM.

'There comes a time in every Salome's life when she should no longer be dropping the last veil.'

Harvey Fierstein

'Wear a hat and some old lady shoes, and you can do whatever you want.'

Elizabeth Berg

WEDDED BLISS

'HOW MANY HUSBANDS HAVE I HAD? YOU MEAN APART FROM MY OWN?'

Zsa Zsa Gabor

'WHEN A MAN RETIRES, HIS WIFE GETS TWICE THE HUSBAND BUT ONLY HALF THE INCOME.'

Chi-Chi Rodriguez

Wife:
I'M AFRAID YOU WON'T LOVE ME NOW THAT MY HAIR HAS TURNED GREY.

Husband:
OF COURSE I WILL – I'VE LOVED YOU THROUGH ALL THE OTHER COLOURS, HAVEN'T I?

ETHEL: HOW ARE YOU GOING TO VOTE IN THE GENERAL ELECTION?

PEGGY: ALL MY LIFE I'VE ALWAYS VOTED THE SAME AS MY HUSBAND.

ETHEL: OH! SO HOW IS HE GOING TO VOTE?

PEGGY: I HAVEN'T DECIDED YET.

'The best way to get most husbands to do something is to suggest that perhaps they're too old to do it.'

Anne Bancroft

'An archaeologist is the best husband a woman can have; the older she gets, the more interested he is in her.'

Agatha Christie

AGED TO PERFECTION

'Is it just me, or are pensioners getting younger these days?'

The Queen Mother

'Ageing seems to be the only available way to live a long life.'

Kitty O'Neill Collins

LITTLE GIRL:
HOW OLD ARE YOU?

OLD LADY:
82!

LITTLE GIRL:
DID YOU START AT 1?

'THE REALLY FRIGHTENING THING ABOUT MIDDLE AGE IS THAT YOU KNOW YOU'LL GROW OUT OF IT.'

Doris Day

'IT'S SAD TO GROW OLD, BUT NICE TO RIPEN.'

Brigitte Bardot

'OLD AGE AIN'T NO PLACE FOR SISSIES.'

Bette Davis

INSTANT BENEFITS

When you join the Old Dears' Club the rewards start straight away. Your membership begins as soon as you start wearing big bauble necklaces, wee a little when you sneeze and send a postal order for half your life savings to a swindling phishing scammer.

AS AN OLD DEAR YOUR INSTANT BENEFITS INCLUDE:

- adding butter to everything.
- wearing too much perfume and jewellery.
- expecting people to be impressed by how old you are.
- doing everything excruciatingly slowly.
- stopping for a coffee or to have a wee twice every hour.
- blaming young people for wasting all their money on lattes and texting.
- eavesdropping on other people's conversations.
- never being criticised for breaking wind.
- slavishly obeying wash care labels except when you send your bath mats to the dry cleaners.
- using a heavy liquid foundation topped off with powder to cover your wrinkles.
- wearing a badly fitting bra.
- disciplining the children of strangers.
- always leaving your umbrella somewhere.

OLDER, NOT WISER

'Well-behaved women seldom make history.'

Laurel Thatcher Ulrich

....

'WISDOM DOESN'T NECESSARILY COME WITH AGE. SOMETIMES AGE JUST SHOWS UP ALL BY ITSELF.'

Tom Wilson

....

YOU'RE NEVER TOO OLD TO LEARN SOMETHING STUPID.

HEALTHY BODY, HEALTHY MIND

I KNEW I WAS GETTING OLD WHEN I REALISED I SAW MORE OF THE DOCTOR THAN I DID OF MY FRIENDS.

YOU KNOW YOU'RE GETTING OLD WHEN PEOPLE NO LONGER VIEW YOU AS A HYPOCHONDRIAC.

DOTTIE: Have you heard that Evadne's seeing a psychiatrist?

MURIEL: Is it because she's highly strung?

DOTTIE: Heavens, no! With all her money, she's rich enough to be psychoneurotic.

DOCTOR: I can't find any reason for your poor health, Mrs Anderson. I'm afraid it must be the drink.

MRS ANDERSON: Not to worry, doctor, I'll come back when you're sober.

'THE BODY IS LIKE A CAR: THE OLDER YOU BECOME THE MORE CARE YOU TAKE OF IT – AND YOU DON'T LEAVE A FERRARI OUT IN THE SUN.'

Joan Collins

I'm wrinkled, saggy and lumpy. **And that's just my left leg.**

WISE WOMEN

'The secret to staying young is to live honestly, eat slowly, and lie about your age.'

Lucille Ball

'I refuse to admit I'm more than fifty-two, even if that does make my sons illegitimate.'

Nancy Astor

'I'M NOT SIXTY, I'M SEXTY.'

Dolly Parton

'I don't have time
to think about age.
THERE ARE SO MANY OTHER THINGS TO DO.'

Ursula Andress

'MY GRANDMOTHER
WAS A VERY TOUGH
WOMAN. SHE BURIED
THREE HUSBANDS,
AND TWO OF THEM
WERE JUST NAPPING.'

Rita Rudner

'ONE OF THE
GREATEST PLEASURES
OF GROWING OLD IS
LOOKING BACK AT
THE PEOPLE YOU
DIDN'T MARRY.'

Elizabeth Taylor

IT'S BETTER TO
ARRIVE LATE THAN
TO ARRIVE UGLY.

LOVE YOUR
NEIGHBOUR – BUT
DON'T GET CAUGHT.

EXPERIENCE IS A
WONDERFUL THING.
IT ENABLES YOU TO
RECOGNISE A MISTAKE
WHEN YOU MAKE
IT AGAIN.

Laugh a lot. That way your wrinkles will be in the right places.

There are plenty of fish in the sea. Just find a good hook.

ONE GOOD TURN GETS MOST OF THE BLANKETS.

IT'S FUN TO LET YOUR HAIR DOWN NOW AND THEN. JUST REMEMBER TO PICK IT UP AGAIN.

IF YOU HAVE TO CHOOSE BETWEEN TWO EVILS, ALWAYS PICK THE ONE YOU HAVEN'T TRIED BEFORE.

HOW DO I KNOW IF I'M AN OLD DEAR?

Most people would agree that old dears tend to share one or more of these qualifications: eccentricity, a need to nurture, being prone to hyperbole, being extremely cardiganed, fragility, enjoying pointless hobbies, restricted mobility and possibly some degree of cognitive impairment.

But what separates an old dear from, for example, an old maid or an old biddy? Old dears have been kicking around the block longer than you think. There's certainly a greater element of frailty, kind-heartedness and eccentricity associated with the word 'dear' and this may be related to its medieval roots.

The word 'deer' was originally broad in meaning and became more specific over time. Nowadays 'deer' just refers those elusive ruminant mammals that we all know and love. However, at some point over the last few centuries the branch split into two, with the other meaning being the 'old dear' who merely grows a moustache or mole hair, rather than antlers, moults all year round and feeds mainly on tinned goods rather than leaves.

By the middle of the eighteenth century an 'old Deere' could also refer to the self-scouring steel plough invented by the American blacksmith John Deere. So old farmers were prone to verbal misunderstandings when trying to locate members of their family.

'Where's the old Deere?'
'She be in the shed, with all the other grubby old tools.'
'How dare ye talk about my wife like that!'
'Sorry, I thought you meant...' etc.

OH DEAR

'AGE IS AN ISSUE OF MIND OVER MATTER. IF YOU DON'T MIND, IT DOESN'T MATTER.'

Mark Twain

DON'T LET OLD AGE GET YOU DOWN - IT'S TOO HARD TO GET BACK UP.

I'm not past my 'youth-by' date just yet.

WHAT WOULD JOAN DO?

The world according to Ms Collins

'EVERY WOMAN SHOULD WEAR MAKE-UP. IT TAKES YEARS OFF.'

'I DON'T NEED A HUSBAND. WHAT I NEED IS A WIFE.'

'YOU CAN'T HELP GETTING OLDER,

but you can help yourself from becoming old and infirm, in mind as well as body.'

'Age is just a number. It's totally irrelevant unless, of course, you happen to be a bottle of wine.'

'IF YOU EAT JUNK, YOU LOOK LIKE JUNK.'

'I don't look my age, I don't feel my age and I don't act my age.'

'I have always tried to live my life with enthusiasm and pleasure.'

BATTLE
OF THE SEXES

Wife: I look fat. Please give me a compliment

Husband: You have perfect eyesight.

'My husband's idea of a good night out is a good night in.'

Maureen Lipman

MABEL: AREN'T YOU WEARING YOUR WEDDING RING ON THE WRONG FINGER?

DOROTHY: YES I AM. I MARRIED THE WRONG MAN.

An old lady was in court for shoplifting a tin of peaches.

The magistrate decided that as it contained four peaches, he would send her to jail for four days.

'WAIT!' shouted her husband. **'SHE STOLE A TIN OF PEAS AS WELL.'**

WHEN IT COMES TO HOUSEWORK, MY HUSBAND AND I SHARE THE JOBS. HE DOES THE UNTIDYING AND I DO THE TIDYING.

WHY DO MEN LIKE SMART WOMEN?

OPPOSITES ATTRACT.

BEMUSED AND BEWILDERED

I'm old enough to make my own decisions. Just not young enough to remember what they are.

Age doesn't make you forgetful. Having way too many stupid things to remember makes you forgetful.

'WHEN I WAS YOUNG I COULD REMEMBER ANYTHING – WHETHER IT HAPPENED OR NOT.'

Mark Twain

I've finally reached the wonder years.

WONDER WHERE MY CAR IS PARKED? WONDER WHERE I LEFT MY GLASSES? WONDER WHAT DAY IT IS?

I'M A WALKING LIBRARY OF FACTS. I'VE JUST LOST MY LIBRARY CARD.

MY MIND ISN'T WHAT IS USED TO BE. EVEN THEN IT WASN'T THAT GREAT.

IT'S HARD TO BE NOSTALGIC WHEN YOU CAN'T REMEMBER ANYTHING.

ECCENTRICITY

It's questionable whether you can be an old dear without deviating from a few cultural norms. Eccentricity is a great way to disguise the fact that you're gradually losing your intellectual and physical faculties, while at the same time making people think you're above average intelligence.

Eccentric old dears can literally get away with murder. Being eccentric is much easier than just wearing purple. Simply dedicate a few hours each day to something that nobody else has thought of. Here are some suggestions to get you started:

- chase a truckle of cheese downhill

- share a Happy Meal with an urban fox

- go quad biking in the local department store

- fly a kite in a storm

- write swear words in bleach on your neighbour's lawn

- leave pieces of paper with film plot spoilers on public transport

- spend six months living on communion wafers

- sell everything you own and then buy it all back again

- keep your face in a jar by the door

- lick an iceberg

- teach sign language to a giraffe

- carry around your favourite tin of baked beans

REBEL
REBEL

'I am not eccentric. It's just that I am more alive than most people. I am an unpopular electric eel set in a pond of catfish.'

Edith Sitwell

'TO BE REALLY GREAT AND INTERESTING, YOU HAVE TO BE A LITTLE CRAZY. I JUST DON'T THINK ONE COMES WITHOUT THE OTHER.'

Drew Barrymore

I'M OLD ENOUGH TO KNOW BETTER. THAT MAKES IT EVEN MORE FUN!

THE EYE OF
THE BEHOLDER

'I will not retire while I've still got my legs and my make-up box.'

Bette Davis

'Wrinkles should merely indicate where smiles have been.'

Mark Twain

'EVEN I DON'T WAKE UP LOOKING LIKE CINDY CRAWFORD.'

Cindy Crawford

'BEAUTIFUL YOUNG PEOPLE ARE ACCIDENTS OF NATURE, BUT BEAUTIFUL OLD PEOPLE ARE WORKS OF ART.'

Eleanor Roosevelt

'I refuse to think of them as chin hairs. I think of them as stray eyebrows.'

Janette Barber

TRAVEL THE WORLD BEFORE YOU LOOK LIKE YOUR PASSPORT PHOTO.

AGE TIPTOES IN ON LITTLE CROW'S FEET.

WELCOME TO MY WORLD

I'VE REALISED IT'S TIME TO STOP SAVING FOR MY OLD AGE.

IF THINGS GET BETTER WITH AGE, THEN I'M APPROACHING MAGNIFICENT.

I've watched so many episodes of *Bargain Hunt* and *Countdown*, I think I'm due an honorary degree in media studies.

I ONLY NEED GLASSES WHEN I'M DRIVING THE CAR. **AND WHEN I'M TRYING TO FIND WHERE I PARKED IT.**

I'm grateful when someone tells me I have lipstick on my teeth.

IT MEANS I STILL HAVE TEETH.

Age is a relative term. All my relatives keep reminding me how old I am.

My mind doesn't just wander. Sometimes it leaves completely.

I SAY
I SAY
I SAY...

How do you make an 80-year-old swear?

Get another 80-year-old to shout, 'Bingo!'.

What's the difference between a pitbull and a menopausal woman?

Lipstick.

FLORENCE: I HAD TO SLAP MY DATE THREE TIMES LAST NIGHT.

LILIAN: GOOD HEAVENS! HE'S OLD ENOUGH TO BEHAVE HIMSELF, ISN'T HE?

FLORENCE: OH YES – I JUST HAD TO SLAP HIM TO KEEP HIM AWAKE.

POLICEMAN: You were travelling at forty miles an hour, madam.

OLD LADY: I can't see how, officer, I haven't been out an hour.

"HEY SANDRA", CALLED JEANNETTE, "LOOK AT MY NEW HEARING AID. I CAN HEAR A PIN DROP!"

"GREAT" EXCLAIMED SANDRA, I WANT A NEW ONE, WHAT TYPE IS IT?"

"FIVE O'CLOCK" CAME THE REPLY.

SCOUTMASTER: WHY DID IT TAKE THREE OF YOU TO HELP THAT OLD LADY ACROSS THE ROAD?

SCOUT: SHE DIDN'T WANT TO GO.

BERT: CAN YOU REMEMBER WHEN WE USED TO CHASE YOUNG GIRLS?

KEN: AH, YES... BUT I CAN'T REMEMBER WHY.

OLD DEAR HOBBIES

You can't call yourself an older dear unless you have at least one hobby that takes up enough of your free time to convince you that you're leading a busy and fulfilling life.

If your hobby keeps you fit (e.g. waterskiing, extreme antique fair shopping) that's a bonus, but your hobby should first and foremost be growing or making something that you could buy more conveniently and cheaply in the shops.

HERE ARE FOUR TOP-NOTCH HOBBY IDEAS:

1. **Collecting.** It doesn't matter what you collect, just so long as your collection has no intrinsic value, either aesthetically or financially.

2. **Adult colouring books.** This infantile pastime provides hours of inconsequential activity; utter vapidity at your fingertips.

3. **Making jam.** This has to be the biggest time-waster ever devised by the over-sixties. First you have to pick your fruit, wash it, boil and stir for hours; collect, store and sterilise empty jars; then finally label and decorate. If you make a mistake at any point, you have to throw everything away and start again.

4. **Scrapbooking.** This exercise in extreme torpidity involves hoarding clutter in just two dimensions. It transforms your box of family photos into a portable collection of national significance with you as its self-appointed curator.

EVERYONE NEEDS A
HOBBY

IF I KNIT FAST ENOUGH, DOES IT COUNT AS AEROBICS?

FINISHING THAT JIGSAW IN THREE MONTHS WAS QUITE AN ACHIEVEMENT – THE BOX SAID 2-5 YEARS.

A policeman sees an old lady driving and knitting at the same time. 'Pull over!' he shouts.

SHE REPLIES, 'NO, CARDIGAN!'

CHEERS!

WINE DOESN'T MAKE US ANY YOUNGER. NEITHER DOES CARROT JUICE. WINE IT IS THEN.

WINE IMPROVES WITH AGE. THE OLDER YOU GET, THE MORE YOU LIKE IT.

'PEOPLE MATURE WITH AGE AND EXPERIENCE.

I HOPE I MORE RESEMBLE A FINE WINE THAN BAD VINEGAR.'

Rick Kaplan

My grandmother's 75 and she's never needed glasses. She's just always drunk straight from the sherry bottle.

I DON'T DRINK ALCOHOL ANY MORE. I DON'T HAVE TO – I GET THE SAME EFFECT JUST BY STANDING UP QUICKLY.

'I'm like old wine. They don't bring me out very often – but I'm well preserved.'

Rose Kennedy

'He has a profound respect for old age – especially when it's bottled.'

Gene Fowler

WILDE WORDS

Thoughts from Oscar Wilde

'No woman should be quite accurate about her age. It looks so calculating.'

'A man's face is his autobiography. A woman's face is her work of fiction.'

'WHEN I WAS YOUNG I THOUGHT THAT MONEY WAS THE MOST IMPORTANT THING IN LIFE; NOW THAT I AM OLD I KNOW THAT IT IS.'

'EXPERIENCE IS SIMPLY THE NAME WE GIVE OUR MISTAKES.'

'Thirty-five is a very attractive age. London society is full of women of the very highest birth who have, of their own free choice, remained **THIRTY-FIVE FOR YEARS.**'

'ALL WOMEN BECOME LIKE THEIR MOTHERS. THAT IS THEIR TRAGEDY. NO MAN DOES, AND THAT IS HIS.'

'THE OLD BELIEVE EVERYTHING, THE MIDDLE-AGED SUSPECT EVERYTHING, THE YOUNG KNOW EVERYTHING.'

DEFINING MOMENTS

WILL: A DOCUMENT THAT TELLS YOUR CHILDREN YOU'VE SPENT THEIR INHERITANCE.

DIPLOMAT: A MAN WHO REMEMBERS A WOMAN'S BIRTHDAY BUT FORGETS HER AGE.

Common sense: **a rare form of intelligence that is slowly being bred out of the human race.**

ARGUMENT: A DISCUSSION THAT STARTS WHEN YOU ARE RIGHT AND ENDS WHEN THE OTHER PERSON REALISES THIS.

BABYSITTING:

A FREE SERVICE GIVEN TO THOSE WITH SOMETHING TO DO IN THE EVENINGS (WHO ASSUME THAT YOU HAVE NOTHING TO DO IN THE EVENINGS).

Dog: the only member of your family that you really like.

Radio: something to ignore while doing the crossword.

HOW TO DRESS
LIKE AN OLD DEAR

SEVEN GOLDEN RULES

1. The elastic waistband is so off the fashion piste that even hipsters won't wear one. Choose comfort over style every time.

2. You don't have to be in Vegas to wear animal prints. You just have to be very young or very old. No one can quite be sure whether leopard print is a fashion disaster or a work of genius, so keep them guessing.

3. Light pastel purple is this decade's must-have colour for old dear coats, hats and blouses.

4. Layering: wear three cardigans during the winter so you can take one off during the summer and feel the benefit.

5. Accessorise with matching sets of jewellery to draw attention away from neck wattle and other unsightly areas that haven't been camouflaged by the gold embroidery on your blouse/sweater.

6. Carry a large, unstructured bag or tote and use a huge brooch to secure a scarf or travel rug to your upper torso.

7. Who says that flower-patterned muumuus are just for lounging around the house? If they were good enough for 1972, now they are even more welcome to hide those extra forty years/pounds.

DRESS SENSE

It's incredible! I only have to hang something in my wardrobe for a couple of months and it shrinks two sizes.

WIFE: DO YOU KNOW, DEAR, I CAN STILL GET INTO THE SAME SKIRTS I WORE BEFORE WE WERE MARRIED THIRTY YEARS AGO!

HUSBAND: I WISH I COULD SAY THE SAME.

ONE OF THE JOYS OF OLD AGE IS THAT YOUR OLD CLOTHES HAVE COME BACK INTO FASHION.

THE JOYS OF
AGEING

WRINKLED WAS NOT ONE OF THE THINGS I WANTED TO BE WHEN I GREW UP.

I USED TO HAVE SENIOR MOMENTS. NOW THEY CAN RUN INTO HOURS.

'CAREFUL GROOMING MAY TAKE TWENTY YEARS OFF A WOMAN'S AGE, BUT YOU CAN'T FOOL A FLIGHT OF STAIRS.'

Marlene Dietrich

'I don't need you to remind me of my age. I have a bladder to do that for me.'

Stephen Fry

MY WORST ENEMY?
GRAVITY.

First I put in my false teeth… then I pop in my hearing aid. At that point I can ask where I left my glasses.

I'm getting into swing dancing. Not on purpose. Some parts of my body are just prone to swinging.

YOU KNOW YOU ARE OLD...

... when you know why it's called 'dialling a number'.

... when you take longer to rest than to get tired.

... WHEN YOU SEE YOUR FIRST CAR IN A MUSEUM AND YOUR FAVOURITE CHILDHOOD TOY ON *ANTIQUES ROADSHOW.*

... WHEN YOU WATCH A RACY LOVE SCENE AND THINK 'OOH, THAT BED LOOKS COMFY.'

... WHEN YOU REMEMBER THE KING'S HEAD ON STAMPS.

... WHEN YOU NO LONGER WANT TO GO OUT FOR CANDLELIT DINNERS - BECAUSE YOU CAN'T READ THE MENU.

... WHEN YOU START LYING ABOUT YOUR CHILDREN'S AGES.

... WHEN YOU REMEMBER ELVIS BEING A BAD INFLUENCE.

TIME FOR YOUR NAP

'I don't feel old – I don't feel anything until noon. Then it's time for my nap.'

Bob Hope

'I've been attending lots of seminars in my retirement. They're called naps.'

Merri Brownworth

DEAR SLEEP

I KNOW WE HAD PROBLEMS WHEN I WAS YOUNGER, BUT I LOVE YOU NOW.

'I LIKE TO WAKE UP FEELING A NEW MAN.'

Jean Harlow

You know you're getting old when people ring you at 9pm and the first thing they ask is,

'DID I WAKE YOU?'

IF I REFUSE TO NAP, IS THAT WHAT'S KNOWN AS RESISTING A REST?

I ALREADY WANT TO TAKE A NAP TOMORROW.

HOW TO TALK LIKE AN OLD DEAR

ANOTHER SIX GOLDEN RULES

1. Hyperbole was invented by old dears. A greedy grandchild should always be admonished with the phrase, 'You'll be sick'. Not only does this undermine their parents, it will also set the child up for an eating disorder in later life.

2. Other variations include 'Don't chew your hair, you'll choke' and 'If you don't stop, a policeman will arrest you/Santa won't bring you any presents'.

3. When expressing the fact that you've used maximum effort in a task, declare you've given it '110 per cent'.

4. Always try to introduce your age or your recent hip replacement surgery into the topic of conversation, with the liberal use of phrases such as 'Since my hip replacement surgery...'.

5. When answering the telephone, state the town followed by your telephone number.

6. Once every five years, shock everyone by swearing loudly.

IT'S HOW YOU TELL 'EM

'Being seventy has its advantages.
I was outspoken before, but now what
have I got to keep quiet about?'

Kirk Douglas

'THE OLDER I GROW, THE MORE I LISTEN TO PEOPLE WHO DON'T TALK MUCH.'

Germain G. Glidden

AT MY AGE, 'GETTING HIGH' MEANS IT'S
TIME FOR MY BLOOD PRESSURE PILLS.

QUESTIONS
FROM THE KIDS

WHEN GOD SAID,
'LET THERE BE LIGHT',
DID YOU FLICK
THE SWITCH?

WHEN YOU WERE
AT SCHOOL WAS
HISTORY CALLED
CURRENT AFFAIRS?

IS YOUR
BIBLE
AUTOGRAPHED?

Were you a waitress at
the Last Supper?

Were you ever mugged
by Robin Hood?

When you were young, was the Dead Sea still alive?

Does your birth certificate have hieroglyphics on it?

IS YOUR NATIONAL INSURANCE NUMBER 1?

ARE YOUR EARS STILL RINGING FROM THE BIG BANG?

IS WILLIAM THE CONQUEROR IN YOUR ADDRESS BOOK?

PROVERBIALLY SPEAKING

Everyone is the age of their heart.

Guatemalan proverb

An old fox is not easily snared.

English proverb

YOUNG MEN MAY DIE, BUT OLD MEN MUST DIE.

English proverb

Young twigs will bend, but not old trees.

Dutch proverb

BECOME OLD EARLY IF YOU WOULD BE OLD LONG.

Latin proverb

BE NOT AFRAID OF GOING SLOWLY, BE AFRAID ONLY OF STANDING STILL.

Chinese proverb

BEFORE 30, MEN SEEK DISEASES; AFTER 30, DISEASES SEEK MEN.

Chinese proverb

BIRTHDAY GIRL

PANIC OVER -
ANOTHER YEAR AND
STILL GORGEOUS!

I CAN'T POSSIBLY
BE 80. I DEMAND
A RECOUNT!

WHEN I TURNED 7
I WAS SO EXCITED.
SO WHY WASN'T
I TEN TIMES AS
EXCITED WHEN I
TURNED 70?

'SO MANY CANDLES ... SO LITTLE CAKE.'

Bob Hope

'SO FAR, THIS IS THE OLDEST I'VE BEEN.'

George Carlin

'FOR YEARS I WANTED TO BE OLDER, AND NOW I AM.'

Margaret Atwood

Birthdays are good for you. The more you have, the longer you live.

Birthdays are nature's way of telling us to eat more cake.

WHY OLD DEARS LIKE YOU
LOVED THE
SEVENTIES

Apart from the rubbish piling up in the streets, the power cuts and everything being coloured orange and brown, the seventies were your salad days, weren't they? Admit it.

1. You knew where you were. Men went out to work and you had dinner waiting for them when they got home.

2. You hardly had to parent because your kids played outside until dark and they were in bed before *Z-Cars*.

3. You didn't have to wear seatbelts.

4. You could smoke everywhere, even in cinemas and churches.

5. You didn't get pestered by your grandchildren to buy a mobile phone because they hadn't been born/invented.

6. Summers were sunny and winters were cold, before climate scientists invented freak weather patterns and global warming.

7. You didn't have to bother with sun block on the beach.

8. Entertaining was easy. Prawn cocktail for starters followed by beef stroganoff or macaroni cheese and chocolate mousse.

9. You had simple pleasures: you owned a house, an avocado bathroom suite, a fondue set and a hostess trolley and that was enough.

THE 1970s
– MY HOW WE LAUGHED

I sent my photograph to a Lonely Hearts Club. They sent it back saying they weren't that lonely.

I wouldn't say our house was damp, but the children went to bed with snorkels.

'MY MOTHER-IN-LAW HAS COME ROUND TO OUR HOUSE AT CHRISTMAS SEVEN YEARS RUNNING. THIS YEAR WE'RE HAVING A CHANGE. WE'RE GOING TO LET HER IN.'
Les Dawson

SHOP 'TIL YOU DROP

Why can they send a probe to Mars, but not make a shopping trolley that goes straight?

Online shopping gives me a reason to live for another 3-5 business days.

'WHOEVER SAID THAT MONEY CAN'T BUY HAPPINESS SIMPLY DIDN'T KNOW WHERE TO GO SHOPPING.'

Bo Derek

You know you're getting old when the most important thing to look for when you're shopping is a bench.

I feel such a failure! I've been shopping for fifty years and I still don't have anything to wear.

'I'M SO OLD THAT I DAREN'T EVEN BUY GREEN BANANAS.'

Bruce Forsyth

WHEN I GET TIRED OF SHOPPING I SIT DOWN – AND TRY ON SHOES.

I NEED SCISSORS TO CUT OPEN THE PACKAGING OF MY NEW PAIR OF SCISSORS...

SAGE ADVICE

DON'T TAKE LIFE TOO SERIOUSLY - YOU'LL NEVER GET OUT OF IT ALIVE.

YOU DON'T STOP LAUGHING BECAUSE YOU GROW OLD. YOU GROW OLD BECAUSE YOU STOP LAUGHING.

In your retirement years, never drink coffee at lunch - it will keep you awake in the afternoon.

'BE CAREFUL ABOUT READING HEALTH BOOKS. YOU MAY DIE OF A MISPRINT.'

Mark Twain

'The follies which a man regrets most in his life are those which he didn't commit when he had the opportunity.'

Helen Rowland

'You can live to be a hundred if you give up all the things that make you want to live to be a hundred.'

Woody Allen

FINDING YOUR INNER
POSITIVE OLD DEAR

It's all very well being old and wrinkly on the outside, but you're not a pukka old dear unless you are a glass half full kind of person. The other sort grow up to be grumpy old biddies.

Being an old dear isn't skin deep, it's a lifestyle choice. Old dears can shuffle quietly into any situation and offer rose-tinted words of comfort. Or they might simply stumble into a hedge or a pond to provide comic relief.

TEN POSITIVE AFFIRMATIONS TO GET YOU IN THE MOOD

1. Little old ladies in wheelchairs with blankets over their legs: retired mermaids.

2. You're only as old as you remember you are.

3. I don't think of my skin as saggy, I think of it as relaxed fit.

4. I'm old enough to know better and young enough to do it anyway.

5. Lids: if I can't open it, I probably don't need it.

6. My happiness does not depend on other people; it depends on tea and cake.

7. I don't gossip: I share my opinions about other people's life choices.

8. The four most beautiful words in my vocabulary: no plans for today.

9. I just put on my compression socks and I'm ready to face anything.

10. I'm not old fashioned, just super retro.

POSITVELY PERKY

'THAT'S NOT A GREY HAIR, HONEY.
THAT'S YOUR SILVER LINING.'

Pamela Price

'DREAM AS IF YOU'LL
LIVE FOREVER.
LIVE AS IF YOU'LL
DIE TODAY.'

James Dean

Be positive – don't let today
be a total waste of make-up.

RIGHT ROYAL OLD DEARS

'A MARRIAGE IS NO AMUSEMENT BUT A SOLEMN ACT, AND GENERALLY A SAD ONE.'

Queen Victoria

'I DON'T DISLIKE BABIES, THOUGH I THINK VERY YOUNG ONES RATHER DISGUSTING.'

Queen Victoria

'LIKE ALL FAMILIES, WE HAVE OUR SHARE OF ECCENTRICITIES.'

Queen Elizabeth II

'Golly, I could do with
£100,000, couldn't you?

I HAD SUCH AN
AWFUL
AFTERNOON
WITH MY BANK
MANAGER SCOLDING
ME ABOUT MY
OVERDRAFT.'

Elizabeth the Queen Mother

'I love life.
That's my secret.'

Elizabeth the Queen Mother

'I have to be seen
to be believed.'

Queen Elizabeth II

IDLE THOUGHTS
OF AN OLD DEAR

Why isn't there a special name for the tops of your feet?

If Barbie is so popular, why do you have to buy her friends?

WHERE IN THE NURSERY RHYME DOES IT SAY HUMPTY DUMPTY'S AN EGG?

WHY ISN'T 'PHONETIC' SPELT THE WAY IT SOUNDS?

WHAT WAS THE BEST THING BEFORE SLICED BREAD?

CAN FAT PEOPLE GO SKINNY-DIPPING?

What's another word for 'thesaurus'?

When it rains, why don't sheep shrink?

TXTS FOR OLD DRS

BFF: Best Friend Fainted

COMD: Choked on my Dentures

FWIW: Forgot Where I Was

DWI: DRIVING WHILE INCONTINENT

MGAD: MY GRANDSON'S A DOCTOR

GGPBL: Gotta Go, Pacemaker Battery Low

WIWYA: WHEN I WAS YOUR AGE

GOML: Get Off My Lawn

BMH: Broke My Hip